W9-DIS-025

EASTER

Food and Entertaining

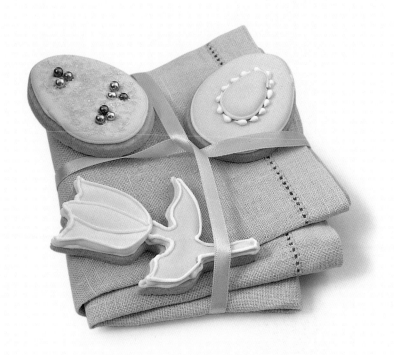

The American Egg Board advises that eggs should not be consumed raw. This book contains dishes made with raw or lightly cooked eggs. It is prudent for more vulnerable people, such as pregnant and nursing mothers, invalids, the elderly, babies and young children to avoid uncooked or lightly cooked dishes made with eggs.

This book includes dishes made with nuts and nut derivatives. It is advisable for customers with known allergic reactions to nuts and nut derivatives and those who may be potentially vulnerable to these allergies, such as pregnant and nursing mothers, invalids, the elderly, babies and children to avoid dishes made with nuts and nut oils. It is also prudent to check the labels of pre-prepared ingredients for the possible inclusion of nut derivatives.

Meat and poultry should be cooked thoroughly. To test if poultry is cooked, pierce the flesh through the thickest part with a skewer or fork—the juice should run clear, never pink or red. Keep refrigerated until ready for cooking.

Pepper should be freshly ground black pepper unless otherwise stated.

Fresh herbs should be used, unless otherwise stated. If unavailable, use dried herbs as an alternative, but halve the quantities stated.

First published in Great Britain in 2003 by

Hamlyn, a division of Octopus Publishing Group Ltd
2–4 Heron Quays, London E14 4JP

ISBN 0 600 60781 X

A CIP catalogue record for this book is available from the British Library

Printed and bound in China

10 9 8 7 6 5 4 3 2

CONTENTS

INTRODUCTION

Think of Easter and plenty of images probably come to mind—frolicking lambs, fluffy chicks, cute bunnies, spring blossoms, daffodils, hot cross buns, and, inevitably, chocolate and Easter eggs. Easter is of great religious significance in the Christian calendar, commemorating the Resurrection of Christ. For many of us, it also means a short vacation—a break from work or school—so, whatever your religious beliefs, it is the ideal time for getting together with friends and family and sharing Easter customs, folklore and eating traditional foods. With its springtime recipes using seasonal produce and its imaginative craft ideas for decorating your home and keeping the children amused, this book is the perfect companion to your festivities.

THE ORIGINS OF EASTER

Easter has its origins in a mix of pagan, Jewish, and early Christian traditions. The word itself is thought to derive from the Old English *eastre*, the name given to a pagan festival held at the spring, or vernal, equinox in honor of the Teutonic goddess of the dawn, Eostre.

Throughout the ancient world, the spring equinox—when night and day are of almost equal length—was a time for celebrating fertility, new life, and regrowth after the winter. Eggs and rabbits or hares, symbolizing this fertility and new life, featured in spring festivals from Egypt to Europe. The Jewish celebration of Passover, which marks the Israelites' flight and freedom from Egyptian slavery, takes place

each spring. Since the Resurrection of Christ occurred during Passover, this was commemorated at the same time of year and also symbolized new life after death. The ancient practices and customs honoring the fertility of the land and its people therefore gradually blended with Christian beliefs to evolve into the religious holiday celebrated as Easter.

EGGS, BUNNIES, AND BASKETS

Today Easter is both a religious holy day and a holiday period during which we enjoy taking part in modern interpretations of customs that have evolved from earlier pagan times.

Easter eggs and the Easter bunny have long had a role to play in the celebrations. Various legends exist to explain the pairing of the two. One describes a bird who wanted to be a rabbit. Granted its wish by the goddess of spring, the grateful creature laid beautiful eggs for her every year. Another recounts how the goddess was saved by a bird whose wings had become frozen during the winter and who had turned into a rabbit. The concept of the egg-providing Easter bunny was brought from Europe to the United States by the Pennsylvania Dutch.

In the past, eggs were brightly painted at Easter to represent spring sunlight and were then given as gifts or used in egg-rolling contests. Nowadays, it is chocolate eggs rather than painted ones that tend to be exchanged, but you and your children can still have

great fun decorating eggs (see pages 52–5). Chic colored eggs hung from branches of pussy willow, another pagan symbol of spring, make a stunning Easter display (see pages 62–3).

Just as Easter itself has mixed origins, so too does the Easter basket. In ancient times, baskets containing the first seedlings and crops were brought to the temple in spring to ensure a good harvest in the fall. A later custom involved carrying the food for Easter dinner to church to be blessed. In the United States, Pennsylvania Dutch children eagerly awaited the 'rabbit's nest' of colorful eggs. The convergence of all these rituals has resulted in the contemporary approach—brightly colored containers filled with candy and other little treats for youngsters at Easter (see pages 56–9 for inspiration).

ENTERTAINING AT EASTER

Joyous and invigorating, spring is often seen as a time for new beginnings and new projects. Since Easter is a celebration of spring and a religious Christian festival, it is the perfect occasion for entertaining family and friends.

Capitalize on the end of cold, dark winters by treating your guests to tasty recipes using the new season's produce. Asparagus and new potatoes are just two of the most eagerly awaited early arrivals (see Steamed Asparagus, page 18, and Celery, Red Onion, and New Potato Salad, page 20). Artichokes too herald the approach of spring (see Mediterranean Stuffed Artichokes, page 28), while lamb, a traditional Easter meal, is another seasonal favorite (see Roast Lamb with Mint Apple Couscous, page 22). The pig has long been a symbol of good luck and prosperity,

so pork (see Apricot Roasted Pork, page 24) is also a popular offering at Easter.

As well as serving these seasonal dishes, together with other Easter goodies such as Hot Cross Buns (see page 8) and Double Chocolate Truffles (see page 46), you could fill the house with the symbols and colors of spring to continue the theme. Arrange simple vases of pussy willow and selections of spring flowers—daffodils, violets, jonquils, crocuses, and tulips—or make an impressive centerpiece for the dining table (see pages 60–61). Stick to spring shades—bright yellows and greens are favorites, or soft pastels—for the best results.

To entertain the children, plan an egg hunt. They will love searching for Easter eggs that have been hidden around the garden—and, of course, chocoholic adults will enjoy the fun too. Encouraging youngsters to make Easter bonnets and supplying hard-boiled eggs for egg-rolling races, like those traditionally enjoyed every year on the lawns of the White House, are other fun ways of keeping the children occupied and at the same time maintaining the old customs.

However you spend your Easter, make the most of this wonderful time of year and enjoy yourselves!

HOT CROSS BUNS

3 cups strong all-purpose
  (bread) flour
$^2/_3$ cup milk
4 tablespoons water
1 oz. fresh yeast or
  2 tablespoons active
  dry yeast
1 teaspoon superfine sugar
1 teaspoon salt
$^1/_2$ teaspoon pumpkin pie
  spice
$^1/_2$ teaspoon ground cinnamon
$^1/_2$ teaspoon grated nutmeg
$^1/_4$ cup superfine sugar
$^1/_2$ stick ($^1/_4$ cup) butter or
  margarine
1 egg, beaten
1 cup currants
$^1/_2$ cup mixed peel, chopped
2 oz. short crust pastry (see
  page 13)

For the glaze
3 tablespoons superfine sugar
4 tablespoons milk and water
  mixed

Makes 12
Preparation time: 1 hour, plus
  standing and rising
Cooking time: 20 minutes

1 Put a quarter of the flour into a small bowl. Warm the milk and water, then blend in the yeast and the teaspoon of sugar. Mix this into the flour and leave in a warm place to froth for about 15 minutes for fresh yeast and about 20 minutes for dry. Meanwhile, sift the remaining flour, salt, spice, cinnamon, nutmeg, and sugar into a mixing bowl.

2 Melt and cool the butter, but do not allow it to harden, then add it to the frothy yeast mixture with the beaten egg. Stir this into the flour and mix well with a wooden spoon. Scatter the currants and candied peel into the mixture and mix to a fairly soft dough. Add a spoonful of water if necessary.

3 Turn the dough onto a floured board and knead well. Put it into an oiled polythene bag and allow to rise for 1–1$^1/_2$ hours at room temperature until doubled in bulk. Turn onto a floured board and knock back the dough. (Knocking back means kneading with your knuckles to knock out the air bubbles and produce a more even texture.)

4 Divide the dough into 12 pieces and shape into small round buns. Press down briefly on each bun with the palm of the hand, then place the buns well apart on a floured baking sheet. Cover and put in a warm place to rise for 20–30 minutes until doubled in size. Meanwhile, roll out the pastry thinly and cut into 24 thin strips about 3$^1/_2$ inches long.

5 When the buns have risen, damp the pastry strips and lay 2 strips across each bun to make a cross. Bake the buns in a preheated oven at 375°F for 20 minutes or until they are golden brown and firm to the touch.

6 Make the glaze by dissolving the sugar in the milk and water mixture over a low heat. When the buns are ready, brush them twice with the glaze, then serve them hot, split, and buttered.

ORANGE POPPY SEED MUFFINS WITH STREUSEL TOPPING

2 1/2 cups all-purpose flour
3 teaspoons baking powder
1/2 cup superfine sugar
1/2 cup poppy seeds
3 eggs
1/2 stick (1/4 cup) butter,
  melted
grated zest and juice of
  1 orange
1/2 cup plain yogurt

For the streusel topping
1/2 cup all-purpose flour
1/4 stick (2 tablespoons) butter
1/4 cup superfine sugar

Makes 12
Preparation time: 20 minutes
Cooking time: 18–20 minutes

These light, fluffy muffins with a hint of orange and a peppering of tiny black poppy seeds are delicious served straight from the oven with a mug of steaming coffee or hot chocolate.

1 To make the streusel topping, put the flour, butter, and sugar into a bowl, then blend with the fingertips until you have rough crumbs. Set aside until later.

2 To make the muffins, put the flour, baking powder, sugar, and poppy seeds into a bowl. Beat the eggs, then add to the bowl with the melted butter, orange zest and juice, and yogurt. Quickly fork together until just mixed.

3 Spoon the mixture into a 12 hole deep muffin pan lined with paper cases. Sprinkle streusel topping over and bake in a preheated oven at 400°F for 18–20 minutes until the muffins are well risen, golden brown, and cracked on the top. Serve warm or at room temperature.

Tips
* The best and lightest muffins are those that are only just mixed together. The more you mix, the heavier they get.
* If you are short of time, top the muffins with crushed sugar lumps or just leave them plain.
* Cooked muffins can be frozen. Warm them in the oven or microwave just before serving.

ORANGE FRENCH TOAST

2 oranges
6 slices raisin bread
2 eggs
4 tablespoons milk
1/4 teaspoon ground cinnamon
1/4 stick (2 tablespoons) butter
2 tablespoons sunflower oil

To serve
4 tablespoons sour cream
2 tablespoons confectioners'
  sugar, sifted

Serves 4
Preparation time: 10 minutes
Cooking time: 10 minutes

1 Pare the zest from one orange using a zester. Using a small serrated knife, peel both oranges, then cut between the membranes to separate the segments. Reserve the zest and segments.

2 Cut the bread slices in half diagonally. Beat the eggs, milk, and cinnamon together in a shallow dish. Heat half the butter and oil in a large sauté pan, then quickly dip half the bread triangles in the egg mixture, turning to cover completely, and add to the pan. Cook in a single layer for 4–5 minutes, turning once, until golden on both sides. Repeat with the remaining butter and oil and bread.

3 Stack three triangles of bread on each serving plate, add sour cream, orange segments, and orange curls, then dust with sugar and serve.

Tip
* If you do not have a zester, use a vegetable peeler and slice the strips of zest into thin ribbons. Soak in iced water until curled, then drain and use as above.

WHOLE-WHEAT CRÊPES WITH MUSHROOMS AND SCALLIONS

½ cup whole-wheat flour

⅔ cup skim milk

1 small egg, beaten

1 teaspoon olive oil

salt and pepper

flat leaf parsley sprigs,
  to garnish

For the filling

1 bunch of scallions, chopped
  fine

1 garlic clove, chopped

4 oz. wild mushrooms, torn

¼ cup low-fat curd cheese

1 tablespoon chopped flat leaf
  parsley

Serves 4
Preparation time: 5 minutes
Cooking time: 35 minutes

1 To make the crêpe batter, place the flour, milk, egg, and salt and pepper in a food processor or blender and process until smooth. Alternatively, you could whisk by hand.

2 Pour a few drops of oil into a skillet. Heat the skillet, pour in a ladleful of batter, and cook for 1 minute. Carefully flip the crêpe and cook the second side, then slide it out onto waxed paper. Make 3 more crêpes in the same way, adding a few drops of oil to the skillet each time, and stack them between sheets of waxed paper.

3 To make the filling, put all the ingredients in a small saucepan and cook, stirring occasionally, for about 5 minutes. Divide between the crêpes, reserving a little, then roll the crêpes up. Transfer them to an ovenproof dish and cook in a preheated oven at 350°F for 20 minutes. Serve with the remaining mixture, garnished with parsley sprigs.

ZUCCHINI, TOMATO, AND BASIL QUICHE

1–2 tablespoons olive oil
1 onion, chopped fine
1 large tomato, skinned,
  deseeded, and chopped
4 basil leaves, chopped fine
8 tiny zucchini, cut into wafer-
  thin slices
2 large eggs
2/3 cup heavy cream
1/2 cup grated mature
  Cheddar cheese
salt and pepper

For the Rich Short Crust
Pastry
3/4 cup all-purpose flour
pinch of salt
1/2 stick (1/4 cup) solid
  block vegetable margarine
  or butter
1/4 stick (2 tablespoons) solid
  block shortening
1 egg yolk
1 tablespoon cold water

Makes 1 large quiche or
  4 individual quiches;
  serves 4
Preparation time: 30 minutes,
  plus chilling
Cooking time: 36–50 minutes

1 First make the pastry. Sift the flour and salt into a bowl. Cut the fats into small pieces and coat with the flour. Blend the fat into the flour until it resembles fine bread crumbs. Mix together the egg yolk and water. Make a well in the center of the flour and add the liquid. Mix with a broad-bladed knife to form a stiff dough, adding a little extra water if necessary. Place in a plastic bag and chill in the refrigerator for about 30 minutes.

2 For the large quiche, roll the pastry into a circle to line a 8 x 1 1/2 inch pan. For the individual quiches, divide the pastry into quarters and roll out into four circles just larger than 4 1/4 x 3/4 inch pans, allowing just enough to cover the base and sides. Press the pastry against the sides of the pan or pans, keeping it an even thickness all the way round. Cut off any excess pastry with a knife.

3 Prick the pastry gently with a fork, line with foil, and fill with pie weights. Place on a baking sheet and bake in a preheated oven at 400°F for 8–10 minutes. Remove the pie weights and foil and bake for a further 8–10 minutes.

4 While the pastry is baking, make the filling. Heat the oil and fry the onion until soft but not colored, then stir in the chopped tomato and basil.

5 Spoon the filling into the cooked quiche shells and arrange the zucchini slices decoratively on top. Reduce the oven temperature to 350°F. Beat the eggs and cream together, add salt and pepper, and pour the mixture over the filling. Sprinkle with grated Cheddar cheese and bake for 25–30 minutes for the large quiche, 20–25 minutes for the individual quiches, until just set and light golden.

WILD MUSHROOM AND HERB OMELET

3/8 stick (3 tablespoons)
  unsalted butter, cut into
  small cubes
2 oz. mushrooms, brushed or
  wiped, trimmed, and sliced
  fine
1 teaspoon finely chopped
  herbs (parsley, chives, and
  chervil)
pinch of all-purpose flour
1–2 tablespoons heavy cream
3 large eggs
salt and pepper
chives, to garnish

Serves 1
Preparation time: 5 minutes
Cooking time: 10 minutes

1 In a small pan (not the omelet pan), melt two-thirds of the butter and fry the mushrooms until they are soft and slightly colored but still hold their shape. Stir in the herbs, flour, and cream, season with salt and pepper, and cook for a few minutes. Remove from the heat and keep warm.

2 Break the eggs into a shallow dish (a soup plate is ideal). Add salt, pepper, and half of the remaining butter. Beat the eggs lightly with a fork, just enough to combine. Warm an 8 inch omelet pan, then put in the remaining butter. When it begins to foam and just before it starts to brown, pour in the eggs. Quickly stir the contents of the pan 2 or 3 times with the flat of the fork so that as much of the mixture as possible is exposed to the heat.

3 When the underside of the omelet has begun to set, pull the edge of the omelet into the center with a fork and tilt the pan at the same time so that the liquid egg can flow toward the hot surface and set. The omelet is cooked when the underside is set but the top is still soft and slightly runny.

4 Spread the filling over the omelet, folding the nearest edge of the omelet into the center using a fork or palette knife. Tilt the pan away from you, slip the fork under the fold and tip the omelet over again, rolling it toward the edge of the pan. Pull the last remaining bit of omelet from the far edge of the pan over the folded section and press down gently to seal. Keep the tilted pan over the heat for a few seconds longer to brown the bottom of the omelet slightly.

5 Tip the pan against the plate, holding it in such a way that the omelet rolls golden side uppermost onto the plate. Draw a small piece of butter over the surface of the omelet to give it a sheen, then serve immediately, garnished with chives.

Spinach and Egg Muffins with Mustard Hollandaise

7 oz. baby spinach

plenty of freshly grated
  nutmeg

1 tablespoon lemon juice

2 egg yolks

1 tablespoon coarse-grain
  mustard

3/4 stick (6 tablespoons) lightly
  salted butter, diced

4 muffins, split

1 tablespoon vinegar

4 eggs

Serves 4
Preparation time: 10 minutes
*Cooking time: about 10
  minutes*

1 Place the spinach and nutmeg in a saucepan and add a tablespoon of water. Set this aside while making the sauce.

2 Place the lemon juice, egg yolks, and mustard in a heatproof bowl over a pan of gently simmering water. Add a piece of the butter and whisk until the butter has melted into the sauce. Continue whisking in the butter, a piece at a time, until the sauce is thickened and smooth (this will take about 5 minutes). If the sauce becomes too thick, whisk in a tablespoon of hot water. Keep the sauce over the simmering water until ready to use.

3 Toast the muffins and keep warm. Place the vinegar in a saucepan with plenty of hot water, bring to the boil and poach the eggs. Cover the spinach pan with a lid and cook for about 1 minute until the spinach has wilted.

4 Transfer the muffins to serving plates, pile them up with spinach, then add the poached eggs, and finally the sauce. Serve immediately.

POTATOES WITH GARLIC AND PANCETTA

4 oz. pancetta, cubed

1 onion, chopped

1¼ lb. potatoes, cubed and
  boiled

2 garlic cloves, minced

1 tablespoon chopped parsley

2 tablespoons freshly grated
  Parmesan cheese

Serves 4

Preparation time: 5–10
  minutes

Cooking time: 12–16 minutes

1 Cook the pancetta in a nonstick skillet for 3–4 minutes until it begins to brown.

2 Add the onion, potatoes, and garlic and continue to fry for 8–10 minutes until the potatoes are browned, then stir in the parsley.

3 Place the mixture in a flameproof dish and sprinkle over the Parmesan. Cook under a preheated hot broiler for 1–2 minutes, until the Parmesan is melted and golden.

STEAMED ASPARAGUS

8 oz. or a large bunch of
   pencil asparagus
$1/2$ stick ($1/4$ cup) butter
2 tablespoons olive oil
6 tablespoons white bread
   crumbs
6 tablespoons freshly grated
   Parmesan cheese
salt and freshly ground black
   pepper
Parmesan shavings, to garnish
   (optional)

Serves 4
Preparation time: 10 minutes
Cooking time: 5 minutes

Always choose pencil-slim tender stems of asparagus for the best taste and top with a sprinkling of crisp sautéed bread crumbs mixed with finely grated Parmesan cheese.

1 Trim the woody ends and 1 inch of green from the bottom of the asparagus stems. Rinse in cold water, drain, and put into the top of a steamer set over a pan of boiling water. Cover and steam for 5 minutes.

2 Meanwhile, heat a quarter of the butter and all the oil in a sauté pan. When hot, add the bread crumbs and cook, stirring, until golden brown and crisp. Add the grated Parmesan and salt and pepper and cook for 1 more minute.

3 Melt the remaining butter in a small pan. Toss the cooked asparagus gently in the butter until it is evenly coated. Spoon onto serving plates and sprinkle with the crisp crumbs. Garnish with shavings of Parmesan if using.

Tips
* Use up leftover bread by making it into bread crumbs in the food processor, then pack into plastic bags and freeze. There is no need to thaw the bread crumbs, just take out as many as you need and add them to the pan. They are great on cheesy pasta dishes too.
* To make Parmesan shavings, run a swivel-bladed vegetable peeler along the side of a block of Parmesan cheese.

CELERY, RED ONION, AND NEW POTATO SALAD

1 lb. new potatoes, halved
1 small fennel bulb, halved,
    cored, and sliced fine
2 celery stalks, sliced thin
1 red onion, halved and
    sliced thin
celery leaves or dill sprigs, to
    garnish (optional)

For the dressing
3/4 cup mayonnaise
2 teaspoons coarse-grain
    mustard
2 tablespoons finely chopped
    dill
salt and pepper

Serves 4
Preparation time: 10 minutes
Cooking time: 10–15 minutes

1 Add the potatoes to a large saucepan of boiling water and boil for about 10–15 minutes until they are tender.

2 Meanwhile, mix the fennel, celery, and onion in a large, shallow bowl and set aside.

3 To make the dressing, mix the mayonnaise, mustard, and dill in a small bowl, adding salt and pepper to taste.

4 Drain the potatoes, rinse under cool running water, and drain again. Add the potatoes to the salad. Pour over the dressing and toss the ingredients until they are well coated. Garnish with celery leaves or dill sprigs if using.

Spring Green Salad

large handful or 2 oz. arugula
  leaves
1 Bibb or round lettuce,
  separated, outer leaves
  discarded
1/4 frisée lettuce
1 avocado
1 tablespoon lemon juice

For the dressing
2 tablespoons balsamic or
  raspberry vinegar
4 tablespoons light olive oil
2 tablespoons finely chopped
  mint
salt and pepper

To garnish
mint leaves (optional)
fresh raspberries (optional)

Serves 4
Preparation time: 15 minutes

Fresh, light, and good enough to eat on its own as a starter, this salad is also great with grilled salmon or chicken breasts, or served with broiled goats' cheese on toast as an alternative to the cheese board. Three different salad leaves have been used here, but a different variety of mixed leaves could be used if preferred.

1 Tear the large salad leaves into bite-sized pieces, put them into a colander, and rinse with cold water. Dry in a salad spinner or pat dry with a clean dish towel.

2 Halve the avocado. Remove the stone and skin, then cut it into thin slices. Toss with lemon juice to prevent discoloration.

3 Mix all the dressing ingredients together in the bottom of a salad bowl. Add the salad leaves and toss together gently. Arrange the avocado slices on top of the leaves in a fan shape and then garnish with tiny mint leaves and raspberries if using.

Tips
* This salad also looks pretty garnished with pansy or viola flowers.
* Serve the salad immediately after making so the leaves stay crisp and the avocado retains its pale-green color.

ROAST LAMB WITH MINT APPLE COUSCOUS

4 lb. leg of lamb
1 tablespoon olive oil for
  roasting

For the marinade
1 cup dry white wine
1 onion, roughly chopped
3 garlic cloves, chopped
2 tablespoons light brown sugar
2 bay leaves
1 teaspoon black peppercorns

For the Mint Apple Couscous
2 cups couscous
5 oz. green beans, sliced thin
2 cups frozen peas
4 tablespoons olive oil
finely grated zest and juice of
  2 lemons
2 red sweet apples, cored
  and diced
4 tablespoons chopped
  mint leaves
salt and pepper

To garnish
lemon wedges
fresh mint sprigs

Serves 6
Preparation time: 30 minutes,
  plus chilling
Cooking time: 1³/₄–2¹/₄ hours

The natural sweetness of new-season roast lamb is unique. Here it is served with a much lighter and more refreshing alternative to roast potatoes: a warm, tangy couscous salad flecked with diced apple, green beans, and peas, bathed in a minty lemon dressing.

1 Rinse the lamb in cold water, pat dry with paper towels, and prick with a fork. Put all the marinade ingredients into a large plastic bag, add the lamb, and seal the bag well. Put it into a large, shallow container or roasting pan and chill in the refrigerator overnight.

2 Take the lamb out of the refrigerator, turn it over in the marinade, and allow to come to room temperature for 1 hour. Remove the lamb from the bag, reserving the marinade, put it into a roasting pan and drizzle with the tablespoon of olive oil. Cook in a preheated oven at 375°F for 25 minutes per 1 lb. for medium, plus an extra 25 minutes for well done, spooning the meat juices over the lamb once or twice during cooking.

3 About 15 minutes before the lamb will be cooked, start to prepare the mint apple couscous. Put the couscous into a bowl and add 4 cups of boiling water. Cook the green beans and peas in a saucepan of boiling water for 4 minutes. Mix together the oil, lemon zest and juice, and salt and pepper in a bowl and stir in the diced apple. Pour off any excess water from the couscous, then stir in the green vegetables, apple, and dressing. Add the chopped mint and toss together.

4 Boil the meat juices together with the marinade for 3 minutes, then strain into a jug to serve at the table. Arrange each serving of the lamb on top of some couscous, and garnish with lemon wedges and sprigs of mint.

Tips
* For a summer version, serve with barbecued butterflied shoulder of lamb.
* If you are not feeding a crowd, reduce the size of the couscous salad and serve with broiled lamb chops or lamb kabobs.

APRICOT ROASTED PORK

3 lb. boned pork loin

2 tablespoons olive oil

1 onion, chopped fine

1 teaspoon fennel seeds,
  roughly crushed

1 1/2 cups fresh white bread
  crumbs

1/2 cup pistachio nuts, roughly
  chopped

3/4 cup (4 oz.) dried apricots,
  roughly chopped

1 egg, beaten

2 tablespoons smooth apricot
  preserve

2 tablespoons all-purpose
  flour

2 1/2 cups chicken or pork
  stock

coarse sea salt and pepper

green beans, to serve

Serves 8
Preparation time: 30 minutes
Cooking time: 1 1/2 hours

Pistachios give an exotic crunch to this delicious pork, while dried apricots add a wonderful sweetness, complemented by just a hint of fennel.

1 Lay the pork out flat on a board with the fat underneath. Make a central cut down the length, just below the eye of the meat, taking care not to go as deep as the fat. Open out the joint so it is the same thickness all the way along.

2 Heat half the oil in a sauté pan, add the onion, and cook until softened. Stir in the fennel seeds, bread crumbs, pistachios, apricots, egg, and salt and pepper, mixing well. Spoon this stuffing evenly over the meat, then roll it up and tie it at intervals with string.

3 Put the pork in a roasting pan, drizzle with the remaining oil, and season with salt and pepper. Bake in a preheated oven at 400°F for 30 minutes per 1 lb., spooning the meat juices and preserve over the pork fat 20 minutes before the end of cooking.

4 Transfer the pork to a serving plate and carve some slices ready to serve. Stir the flour into the pan juices, cook for 2 minutes, then gradually mix in the stock. Season and bring to a boil, stirring, then strain into a gravy jug to take to the table with the pork. Serve with green beans, if using.

HONEY ROASTED HAM

4 lb. smoked ham joint,
   soaked in cold water
   overnight
1 onion, chopped
1 carrot, sliced
3 bay leaves
1 teaspoon black peppercorns
1 tablespoon whole cloves
2 tablespoons clear honey
2 teaspoons coarse-grain
   mustard
1/2 teaspoon ground cloves
1/4 teaspoon paprika (optional)

Serves 8
Preparation time: 10–15
   minutes
Cooking time: 2 hours

This moist baked ham is glazed with a mixture of honey, coarse-grain mustard, and cloves. It is equally good served hot with spring vegetables or cold with poached eggs for a lazy brunch.

1 Drain the ham joint and put into a roasting pan with the onion, carrot, bay leaves, and peppercorns. Pour on enough boiling water to come halfway up the sides of the roasting pan, then cover the joint and pan with foil, twisting the edges around the rim of the pan.

2 Bake in a preheated oven at 350°F for 25 minutes per 1 lb. Remove the foil, cut away the rind, then mark a criss-cross grid with a knife. Press the whole cloves into the fat. Mix together the honey, mustard, ground cloves, and pimentón. Spoon over the ham fat so that it is completely covered, then return the ham to the oven, uncovered, and cook for 20 minutes until the fat is golden.

3 Transfer the ham to a serving plate. Strain the pan juices into a gravy jug and serve with the meat thinly sliced, hot or cold.

Tip
* If the fat seems to be browning unevenly, shield those areas that are browned with strips of foil and return to the oven until the rest is the same color.

GRILLED CHICKEN WITH LEMON AND ARTICHOKES

4 boneless, skinless chicken
    breasts, about 8 oz. each
3 tablespoons all-purpose flour
3 tablespoons olive oil
grated zest of 1 and juice of
    2 lemons
13 oz. can artichoke hearts,
    drained
4 tomatoes, peeled,
    quartered, and diced
small bunch of basil or chervil
salt and pepper

Serves 4
Preparation time: 25 minutes
Cooking time: 12 minutes

This is quick and easy to put together yet impressive enough to serve to friends, accompanied by tiny new potatoes, steamed green beans or asparagus, and a good bottle of chilled white wine.

1 Rinse the chicken breasts in cold water, then drain well. Put each breast between 2 sheets of saran wrap and pound with a rolling pin until doubled in size, then cut into 2 or 3 pieces. (You can leave them whole if preferred.)

2 Mix the flour and salt and pepper on a plate, then use to coat the pieces of chicken breast. Heat the oil in a large grill pan and add the chicken. Cook for 5 minutes, turning until browned all over and cooked through.

3 Add the lemon zest and juice, halved artichokes, and tomatoes to the pan with the chicken, and cook for 2 minutes. Sprinkle with herb leaves and serve immediately.

Tip
*You could also serve this with cooked wild or long-grain white rice.

CRAB AND SWEET POTATO CAKES

1 lb. sweet potatoes

8 oz. boiling potatoes

1 small egg, beaten

8 oz. crabmeat

1/2 teaspoon paprika

3 tablespoons all-purpose
flour

oil, for shallow-frying

salt and pepper

salad leaves, to serve

For the Aioli

2 garlic cloves, minced

1 small red chile, seeded and
chopped

1 medium egg yolk

1 tablespoon white wine
vinegar

2/3 cup olive oil

Serves 4

*Preparation time: 15 minutes,
plus chilling*

Cooking time: 22–26 minutes

1 Peel both types of the potatoes and cook in boiling water for about 10 minutes or until soft when pierced with the tip of a knife. Drain well, return to the pan, and roughly mash.

2 Add the beaten egg, season with salt and pepper, and mix well. Add the crabmeat and mix into the potato mash with the paprika and flour.

3 With floured hands, shape 2 tablespoons of the mixture into a potato cake. Repeat until all the mixture has been used, then chill in the refrigerator for 1–2 hours.

4 Heat the oil in a large skillet and fry 4 potato cakes at a time for 3–4 minutes, turning occasionally, until they are golden brown on all sides and heated through. Remove from the oil and drain well. Keep warm while cooking the remainder.

5 To make the aioli, put the garlic and chile in a food processor or blender with the egg yolk and vinegar and process well. With the motor still running, slowly add the olive oil in a thin stream. If it is added slowly enough, the egg mixture will gradually thicken into a mayonnaise.

6 Serve the warm potato cakes with large spoonful of the aioli and a mixture of crisp salad leaves.

MEDITERRANEAN STUFFED ARTICHOKES

2 whole globe artichokes

4 slices or 3 oz. French bread

2 garlic cloves, halved

4 tablespoons olive oil

1 tablespoon red wine vinegar

1 teaspoon sun-dried tomato
paste (optional)

3 tomatoes, skinned, seeded,
and diced

2 teaspoons capers

salt and pepper

basil leaves, to garnish
(optional)

Serves 4

Preparation time: 15–20
minutes

Cooking time: 25 minutes

This eye-catching vegetable is surprisingly easy to cook and makes a delicious appetizer served warm with an Italian-inspired tomato and caper salad dotted with crisp garlicky croutons.

1 Trim the artichoke stalks close to the base, then cook them in a large saucepan of salted water for 25 minutes or until you can easily pull a leaf away from the base. Drain well.

2 Meanwhile, toast the bread slices on both sides, then rub with garlic. Finely chop the remaining garlic and mix with the oil, vinegar, tomato paste, if using, and salt and pepper. Stir in the tomatoes and capers.

3 Halve the artichokes, cutting down through the top to the stalk at the base. Scoop out the hairy choke from the center using a teaspoon. Arrange a half per portion, cut side uppermost, on serving plates. Finely dice the bread, then stir into the tomato mixture and spoon this beside the artichokes. Garnish with basil, if using.

4 Serve warm, tearing off artichoke leaves and dunking them in the tomato salad before nibbling the soft flesh from the end of each leaf.

LIME CHEESECAKE WITH BERRIES

½ stick (¼ cup) butter
2 tablespoons corn syrup
5 oz. graham crackers,
  crushed

For the filling
1 cup mascarpone cheese
¾ cup virtually fat-free
  fromage frais
¼ cup superfine sugar, sifted
grated zest and juice of
  2 limes
½ cup heavy cream

To decorate
8 oz. strawberries, halved or
  sliced if large
4 oz. blueberries
sifted confectioners' sugar
  (optional)

Serves 4
Preparation time: 15–20
  minutes, plus chilling
Cooking time: 5 minutes

This cheesecake is a perfect after-dinner dessert as it doesn't need any baking and can easily be made in advance, leaving you more time to entertain.

1 To make the base, melt the butter and syrup in a saucepan. Put the crackers in a plastic bag and crush them finely with a rolling pin, then tip them into the butter mixture and stir well. Press them into the base of an 7 inch loose-bottomed, fluted flan pan.

2 Beat the mascarpone in a bowl to soften, then stir in the fromage frais, sugar, and lime zest. Gradually beat in the lime juice.

3 In a second, smaller bowl, whisk the cream until it forms soft peaks, then fold into the mascarpone mixture. Spoon the creamy filling onto the biscuit base and swirl the top with the back of a spoon. Chill for 3 hours, or longer if preferred.

4 Carefully remove the cheesecake from the pan and decorate with berries and a dusting of confectioners' sugar if using.

HOT BERRY SOUFFLÉS

1 tablespoon butter
1/2 cup superfine sugar
2 oz. blackberries
7 oz. raspberries
4 large egg whites
confectioners' sugar, to dust
custard or ice cream, to serve
   (optional)

Serves 4
Preparation time: 15 minutes
Cooking time: 15 minutes

1 Use the butter to grease four 1 cup ramekins and then coat them evenly with a little of the superfine sugar, tipping out any excess. Place the ramekins on a baking sheet.

2 Purée the blackberries and raspberries in a food processor or blender, reserving a few of the berries to decorate, then pour the purée into a bowl. Alternatively, the fruit can be rubbed through a fine sieve to make a smooth purée.

3 Place the egg whites in a large, perfectly clean bowl, then use an electric beater to whisk them until they are stiff but not dry. Gradually sprinkle in the remaining superfine sugar, continue to whisk. Carry on whisking until the whites are stiff and shiny.

4 Gently fold the egg whites into the berry purée, then spoon this mixture into the prepared ramekins. Bake immediately in a preheated oven at 375°F for 15 minutes or until risen and golden.

5 Dust the soufflés with confectioners' sugar and decorate with the reserved berries. Serve immediately, with custard or ice cream if using.

LAVENDER CRÈME BRÛLÉE

2¹/₂ cups light cream
4–6 lavender flowers,
   depending on size
6 egg yolks
¹/₃ cup superfine sugar
6 teaspoons raw brown sugar
fresh lavender, to decorate

Serves 6
Preparation time: 15 minutes,
  plus infusing and chilling
Cooking time: 35–40 minutes

Lavender is rarely used in cooking nowadays but it can add a delicate perfume to recipes and can also make an ideal theme for a table decoration.

1 Pour the cream into a small saucepan, add the lavender flowers and gently heat for 2–3 minutes, but do not boil. Take off the heat and allow to infuse for 30 minutes.

2 Beat the egg yolks and sugar together until smooth. Take the lavender out of the cream with a draining spoon and then reheat the cream, bringing it almost up to a boil. Gradually stir the hot cream into the egg yolk mixture and then strain into a jug or back into the saucepan. Pour into 6 individual ovenproof ramekins or shallow dishes, cover the tops with foil and stand them in a roasting pan. Pour in enough cold water to come halfway up the sides of the dishes and then bake in a preheated oven at 325°F for 25–30 minutes until just set.

3 Take the dishes out of the roasting pan and cool at room temperature, then chill for at least 4 hours or overnight in the refrigerator. Sprinkle raw brown sugar over the tops of the dishes and cook under a preheated broiler or using a flame torch for 3–5 minutes until the sugar has caramelized. Chill and serve decorated with fresh lavender within 30 minutes.

Tips
* If the caramel topping is left too long after making, it will begin to soften and lose its wonderful crunchy texture.
* If you have a slow broiler, you may like to stand the chilled dishes in a roasting pan or on the base of a broiler pan filled with ice so that the cream layer stays cold while the sugar melts.
* Brûlée is also delicious served with blueberries and tiny strawberries.

Honey Pears with Minted Mascarpone Cream

1/4 stick (2 tablespoons) butter
2 tablespoons runny honey
4 ripe pears, such as Red
  William, peeled, cored, and
  sliced lengthways
a little lemon juice

For the Minted Mascarpone Cream
1 tablespoon finely chopped
  mint
1 tablespoon superfine sugar
3/4 cup mascarpone cheese

To decorate
confectioners' sugar
ground cinnamon

Serves 4
Preparation time: 10 minutes
Cooking time: 7 minutes

1 Melt the butter in a small saucepan. Remove from the heat and stir in the honey. Mix well.

2 Sprinkle the pear slices with lemon juice as soon as they are prepared to prevent discoloration. Line a baking sheet with foil and lay the pear slices on it. Then brush with the butter and honey mixture. Heat the broiler to the hottest setting and broil the pears for 5 minutes.

3 Meanwhile, make the minted mascarpone cream by lightly whisking the chopped mint and sugar into the mascarpone cheese.

4 To serve, divide the pear slices between 4 plates and add a dollop of the minted mascarpone cream to each. Lightly dust with confectioners' sugar and ground cinnamon, then serve immediately.

CRÊPES SUZETTE

For the crêpes
1¹/₂ cups all-purpose flour
a pinch of salt
1 egg, lightly beaten
1¹/₄ cups milk
light olive oil, vegetable oil, or
    butter, for greasing pan

For the sauce
¹/₂ stick (¹/₄ cup) butter
¹/₄ cup superfine sugar
grated zest and juice of
    2 oranges
2 tablespoons Grand Marnier
2 tablespoons brandy
sour cream, to serve

Serves 4
Preparation time: 15 minutes
Cooking time: 25–35 minutes

1 To make the crêpes, put the flour and salt in a bowl and make a well in the center. Pour the egg and some of the milk into the well. Whisk the liquid, gradually incorporating the flour to make a smooth paste. Whisk in the remaining milk, then pour the batter into a measuring cup with a pouring spout.

2 Put a little oil or butter into a 7 inch crêpe pan or heavy-based skillet and heat until it starts to smoke. Pour off the excess and pour a little batter into the pan, tilting it until the base is coated with a thin layer. Cook for 1–2 minutes until the underside begins to turn golden.

3 Flip the crêpe with a spatula and cook for a further 30–45 seconds until it is golden on the second side. Make the remaining crêpes in the same way. Set them aside while preparing the sauce to accompany them.

4 Melt the butter in a skillet, add the sugar, orange zest and juice, and heat until bubbling. Dip each crêpe into the sauce, then fold it into quarters and place on a warmed serving dish.

5 Add the Grand Marnier and brandy to the skillet, heat gently, then ignite. Pour the flaming liquid over the crêpes and serve immediately with sour cream.

LEMON ANGEL FOOD CAKE

½ cup all-purpose flour
finely grated zest of ½ lemon
6 egg whites
pinch of salt
¾ teaspoon cream of tartar
1 cup superfine sugar
crystallized rose petals or
   flowers, to decorate
   (optional)

For the frosting
½ cup lemon curd
½ cup sour cream

Serves: 8
Preparation time: 30 minutes
Cooking time: 25 minutes

This light, spring-like cake is the perfect way to end a special Easter meal. If you are pressed for time you could always make the cake a couple of days in advance, freeze it and simply add the frosting as it thaws.

1 Sift the flour onto a plate, then stir in the lemon zest and set aside.

2 Put the egg whites, salt, and cream of tartar into a large bowl and whisk until you have stiff but moist-looking peaks. Gradually whisk in the sugar, a tablespoonful at a time, and continue whisking for 1–2 minutes.

3 Gently fold in the flour and lemon zest using a metal spoon and a swirling figure-of-eight action. Pour into a 8 inch deep or 9 inch shallow nonstick angel cake pan (there is no need to grease it first). Bake in a preheated oven at 375°F for 25–30 minutes until well risen and golden and the top springs back when pressed with a fingertip.

4 Turn the cake, still in its pan, upside-down onto a cooling rack and leave to cool. As it cools it will fall out of the pan. When cold, mix the lemon curd and sour cream together and spread over the top of the cake. Sprinkle with crystallized rose petals or flowers if using (see right).

Tips
* To crystallize flowers, buy a sachet of dried egg white and mix it as instructed. Let it cool, then brush it over rose petals or viola, pansy, or herb flowers. Dust lightly with a little superfine sugar, leave to dry for 30 minutes, then add to the cake just before serving.

SIMNEL CAKE

1½ sticks (¾ cup) butter or
   margarine
¾ cup superfine sugar
3 large eggs, lightly beaten
1½ cups all-purpose flour
1 teaspoon ground cinnamon
1 teaspoon grated nutmeg
2½ cups currants
¾ cup golden raisins
½ cup chopped candied peel
1–2 tablespoons milk
1 lb. marzipan
3–4 tablespoons apricot
   preserve
1 egg, beaten, for glazing

Serves: 10
Preparation time: 25 minutes
Cooking time: 3 hours

1 Line a 7 inch round cake pan.
Cream the butter and sugar and beat
in the eggs a tablespoon at a time,
mixing well between each addition.
Sift the flour with the spices and fold
this in, followed by the fruit. Mix to a
soft consistency with a little milk. Put
half the mixture into the prepared tin
and level it off.

2 Divide the marzipan into 3 and roll
out one-third into a round slightly
smaller than the pan. Pinch the edges
to prevent the paste cracking. Lay the
round on the cake mixture, place the
other half of the cake mixture on top,
and level it off. Tie a band of brown
paper round the outside of the pan to
come 2 inches above it, to protect the
top of the cake during baking. Put it in
the center of a preheated oven at
325°F and bake for 1 hour. Reduce the
heat to 300°F and cook for a further
2 hours or until the cake is firm to the
touch. Allow to cool in the pan before
removing the lining paper and turning
out onto a wire rack to cool.

3 Heat the preserve and sieve if
lumpy. Roll out a reserved piece of
marzipan into a round for the cake top.
Brush the apricot glaze over the cake
top and press on the marzipan. Pinch
the edges of the marzipan into flutes.

4 Flatten the remaining marzipan and
divide into 11 equal parts. Roll each
one into a small ball. Brush the top and
sides of the marzipan on the cake with
beaten egg. Press on the balls round
the edge of the cake. Glaze with beaten
egg, then brown under a hot broiler.

5 When the cake is cool, it can be
wrapped in foil and stored for at least
2 weeks.

COLUMBA CAKE

1¼ cups hand-hot water

¼ cup superfine sugar

1 tablespoon active dry yeast

4½ cups strong all-purpose
(bread) flour

2 eggs, beaten

¾ stick (6 tablespoons) butter,
at room temperature

1 cup golden raisins

½ cup dried cranberries

2 pieces (3 oz.) citron peel,
diced

grated zest of 1 lemon

To decorate

1 cup confectioners' sugar

2 tablespoons fresh lemon
juice

small piece (1 oz.) lime
citron peel

Serves 12

Preparation time: 30 minutes,
plus rising

Cooking time: 25–30 minutes

Traditionally this rich, buttery fruit bread is made in the shape of a dove (which explains its name, as 'columba' is Latin for dove) and served with coffee after Easter Sunday lunch. The dove is associated with fertility and rebirth, so it also symbolizes the Resurrection of Christ. This cake can also be made with a plain, round springform pan.

1 Pour the water into a bowl and stir in 1 teaspoon of sugar. Sprinkle the yeast over the top and leave in a warm place for 5–10 minutes until the yeast has formed a frothy head about ¾ inch thick.

2 Put the flour into a large warmed bowl, add the yeast mixture and eggs, and mix to a smooth dough. Turn out onto a work surface dusted with a little more flour and knead well for 5 minutes until smooth and elastic. Put the dough back in the bowl, cover with a plate or oiled saran wrap, and leave in a warm place for about 40 minutes or until doubled in size.

3 Knead the dough on the work surface as before. Flatten it slightly, then spread with about a third of the butter. Mix the dried fruits, peel, and lemon zest together and sprinkle a third over the dough. Fold the dough over and knead flat again. Repeat with the butter and fruit until all has been added. Press the dough into a buttered 9 inch deep loose-bottomed cake pan.

4 Cover as before and leave to rise for about 40 minutes until the dough reaches the top of the pan. Bake in a preheated oven at 400°F for 25–30 minutes until the bread is golden brown and sounds hollow when tapped with the fingertips. Remove from the oven and leave in the pan for 5 minutes.

5 Mix most of the confectioners' sugar to a smooth, thin paste with the lemon juice. Cut the peel into very thin strips. Take the bread out of the pan and put on a cooling rack. Sprinkle the peel over the top, then drizzle with confectioners' sugar and leave to cool. Cut into thick slices to serve.

Tip
* If you are unsure about getting the right temperature for the water to froth the yeast, use 1 part boiling to 2 parts cold.

EASTER NEST TORTE

½ cup self-rising flour

½ teaspoon baking powder

⅓ cup cocoa powder

1 stick (½ cup) unsalted
  butter, softened

½ cup superfine sugar

2 eggs

4 tablespoons orange-flavored
  liqueur or orange juice

3 oz. semi-sweet chocolate,
  broken into pieces

For the filling

2 teaspoons powdered gelatin

2 tablespoons cold water

3 egg yolks

¼ cup superfine sugar

1 teaspoon cornstarch

1¼ cups milk

7 oz. semi-sweet chocolate

1¼ cups whipping cream

To decorate

5 oz. milk chocolate at room
  temperature

small chocolate eggs

Serves 12

*Preparation time: 30 minutes,
  plus standing and chilling*

Cooking time: 30 minutes

1 Grease a 9 inch springform pan and line the base. Sift the flour, baking powder, and cocoa into a bowl. Add the butter, sugar, and eggs, then whisk until creamy. Turn into the prepared pan, level the surface, and bake in a preheated oven at 350°F for 20–25 minutes until just firm. Remove from the pan and place on a cooling rack. Move the cake to a serving plate and drizzle with liqueur.

2 Measure the cake's circumference, then cut a waxed paper strip ½ inch longer and 2½ inches wide. Melt the chocolate and spoon it along the strip, spreading it to the edge on one side and shaping a wavy line on the other about ¾ inch from the edge. Leave ½ inch free at one end. Set aside for 15 minutes, then carefully lift the paper strip and secure it round the sponge so the straight chocolate edge rests on the plate and the ends of the strip just meet. Chill.

3 To make the filling, sprinkle the gelatin over the water in a small bowl and allow to soften. Beat the egg yolks in a bowl with the sugar, cornstarch, and a little of the milk. Put the remaining milk in a heavy-bottomed saucepan and bring just to a boil. Pour it over the egg yolk mixture, whisking well. Return the mixture to the saucepan and cook gently, stirring, until thickened. Do not allow to boil.

4 Remove from the heat and stir in the gelatin until dissolved. Break the semi-sweet chocolate into pieces, add it to the gelatin mixture and leave to melt. Stir until smooth, then turn into a bowl and cover with waxed paper to stop a skin forming. Allow to cool until just beginning to thicken, then remove the paper.

5 Whip the cream to soft peaks and fold into the chocolate mixture. Turn into the chocolate mould on the sponge and level the surface. Chill for 1–2 hours until set. Remove the waxed paper strip.

6 Using a sharp knife, slice the milk chocolate into long, thin shards. If it breaks into brittle pieces, soften it very briefly in the microwave. Lay the shards on top of the cake to create a nest. Pile the eggs in the center to decorate. Chill until ready to serve.

EASTER CUPCAKES

1 cup all-purpose flour
3/4 cup superfine sugar
3/4 cup soft margarine
1 1/2 teaspoons baking powder
1 1/2 teaspoons vanilla extract
2 eggs

For the topping
1 cup confectioners' sugar,
   sifted
1/2 teaspoon vanilla extract
4 teaspoons water
a few drops of yellow, green,
   and pink food coloring
selection of jelly beans, to
   decorate

Makes 12
Preparation time: 20 minutes,
   plus setting
Cooking time: 15–18 minutes

These easy cupcakes are great to make with children. For something a little more adult, add thin slivers of pastel-colored sugared almonds.

1 Put all the cupcake ingredients into a bowl and beat with a wooden spoon or electric mixer until smooth. Spoon into 12 moulds in a muffin pan. Bake in a preheated oven at 350°F for 15–18 minutes until well risen and the cakes spring back when gently pressed with a fingertip. Cool in the pan.

2 For the topping, mix together the confectioners' sugar, vanilla, and enough water to make a smooth frosting. Divide the frosting between 3 bowls and color each batch. Take the cakes out of the pan, frost them, and decorate with jelly beans. Leave for 30 minutes for the frosting to set.

EASTER COOKIES

2 cups all-purpose flour

1/4 cup cornstarch

1 1/2 sticks (3/4 cup) butter, diced

1/2 cup superfine sugar

a few drops of vanilla extract

To decorate

1/2 sachet dried egg white or the equivalent of 1 egg white

2 cups confectioners' sugar, sifted

1 teaspoon lemon juice

selection of liquid or paste food colorings

Makes 18

Preparation time: 20 minutes

Cooking time: 10 minutes

Children will love helping you to make these light, buttery cookies. You can let your imagination run away with you when it comes to decorating them, and be as bold or as restrained as you feel.

1 Put the flour and cornstarch into a bowl and add the butter. Blend with the fingertips or an electric mixer until you have fine crumbs. Stir in the sugar and vanilla until mixed, then bring the mixture together with your hands and squeeze into a smooth ball.

2 Knead lightly, then roll out thinly on a floured surface or a large piece of floured waxed paper if preferred. Stamp out festive shapes using a cutter and transfer to ungreased baking sheets. Reroll the cookie trimmings and continue stamping and rerolling until all the dough is used up.

3 Prick the cookies with a fork, then bake in a preheated oven at 350°F for 10 minutes or until pale golden. Leave to cool on the baking sheet.

4 To make the frosting, mix the dried egg white with water as the sachet directs. Gradually mix in the confectioners' sugar and lemon juice to give a smooth consistency. Add extra water if the frosting seems too thick. Divide between 2 or more bowls and color to taste.

5 Spoon into paper piping bags, snip off the tips, and pipe on the frosting outlines around the edge of the cookie. Leave to dry. Then, fill in the rest of the surface of the cookie with the same color frosting to create a smooth evenly covered cookie top. Leave to dry. Finally, pipe white frosting over the top of the colored surface to outline and make specific features.

Tips

* Eat within 24 hours or the frosting will make the cookies soft.

* Add colored candy for further decoration, if desired.

DOUBLE CHOCOLATE TRUFFLES

1 cup heavy cream
7 oz. luxury semi-sweet
   cooking chocolate
3–4 tablespoons brandy
   or rum

To finish
2 tablespoons cocoa powder
7 oz. luxury dark chocolate
a few crystallized violets
foil petit four moulds

Makes 24
Preparation time: 45 minutes,
   plus chilling
Cooking time: 8 minutes

Wonderfully indulgent, these truffle Easter eggs will make a beautiful gift to present to the host of a special Easter gathering.

1 Pour the cream into a small saucepan and bring to a boil. Take the pan off the heat and break in the semi-sweet chocolate. Leave to stand until it has melted, then stir in the brandy and mix until smooth. Chill for 4 hours until the truffle mixture is firm.

2 Line a baking sheet with waxed paper and dust with sifted cocoa. Scoop a little truffle mixture onto a teaspoon, then transfer it to a second spoon and back to the first again, making a well-rounded egg shape. Slide the truffle onto the cocoa dusted paper. Repeat until all the mixture is used up. Chill again for 2 hours, or overnight if possible, until firm.

3 Break the dark chocolate into a bowl and melt over a saucepan of just-boiled water. Stir well, then, holding one truffle at a time on a fork over the bowl, spoon melted chocolate over the top to coat. Place the truffles on a fresh piece of waxed paper on a baking sheet. Pipe or swirl a little chocolate over the top of each with a spoon and complete with a crystallized violet. Chill for at least 1 hour, then pack into petit four moulds and arrange in little boxes lined with purple tissue paper.

BANANA ORANGE SMOOTHIE

1 ripe banana
2 oranges
1 lime
a handful of ice cubes
½ cup plain yogurt

Serves 2
Preparation time: 10 minutes

Packed with fruit, this is the perfect energy-booster for those who want something light and refreshing.

1 Thickly slice the banana and squeeze the juice from the oranges and lime. Put them in a blender along with the ice cubes and blend until smooth.

2 Add the yogurt and blend again briefly until everything is well mixed together.

3 Pour into 2 tall glasses and serve immediately.

MIMOSA COCKTAIL

1½ cups fresh orange juice,
  chilled
25 fl oz. bottle dry
  Champagne, chilled
fresh mimosa, to decorate

Serves 6
Preparation: 5 minutes

This cocktail will go down well with guests at any time of the day. A crisp sparkling white wine such as Saumur is a good alternative to Champagne.

1 Make sure that both the orange juice and the Champagne are well chilled, then divide the juice between 6 Champagne flutes and top up with Champagne.

2 Arrange the glasses on a tray and decorate this with sprigs of fresh mimosa before serving.

RASPBERRY CHAMPAGNE COCKTAIL

4 oz. fresh raspberries

3 tablespoons crème de
cassis

25 fl oz. bottle dry
Champagne, chilled

4–6 teaspoons grenadine
syrup (optional)

Serves 6
Preparation time: 5 minutes,
plus macerating

Fresh raspberries macerated in crème de cassis and then bathed in chilled champagne,
with just a hint of grenadine for extra flavour, make this a sumptuous and eye-catching
aperitif for a special meal.

1 Put the raspberries in a small bowl
with the crème de cassis and leave to
macerate for at least 30 minutes.

2 Divide the raspberries between
6 Champagne flutes and top up with
well chilled Champagne.

3 Add grenadine to taste, if using, and
serve immediately.

DECORATING EGGS

To Blow Eggs
eggs
large needle
drinking straw
bowl
warm soapy water
paper towels

To Paint Eggs
poster paint, acrylics or
   gouache
eggs
wooden skewer
paint brush

To Dye Eggs
food dye in desired color
boiling water
lemon juice or vinegar
paper towels

The practice of coloring and eating eggs at the spring festival dates back to ancient times. In England in the Middle Ages, Easter Eve was the time when traveling players would perform morality plays, receiving gifts of money, fruit, and hard-boiled eggs, known as 'Pace Eggs', for their trouble. These eggs were dyed various colors using vegetable skins, bark, flowers, and herbs, red being the most popular color. Later, more elaborate effects were achieved by wrapping flowers and ferns around the egg before dyeing it, and in some cases names and little messages were written on the shell too.

TO BLOW EGGS

Before you start to think about how to decorate your eggs, you must first remove their contents, leaving just empty shells. To do this, pierce the top and bottom of each egg with a large needle, the sort you might use for quilting or darning. Working firmly but gently, insert the needle at one end and wiggle it around a little to create a slightly larger hole. Repeat at the other end of the egg, lining up your second hole underneath the first. Then, using a drinking straw, softly blow out the contents into a bowl. When the egg is empty, wash out the inside of the shell with warm soapy water and rinse thoroughly. Allow to drain on paper towels until completely dry before decorating. It is also possible to buy egg-blowing kits from craft shops or catalogs.

TO PAINT EGGS

If you decide to paint your eggs, work out your color scheme and any patterning first. You can use different sorts of paint: experiment with poster paint, acrylics, and gouache. When you are happy with your design, thread an egg onto a wooden skewer and apply your base color. When this coat is dry, apply your pattern in a contrasting color.

TO DYE EGGS

Alternatively, you could dye your eggs. For each different color, mix food dye and boiling water together in a small bowl or cup, then add a splash of lemon juice or vinegar to fix. Add the egg and leave it in the solution for 10 minutes or until you have the depth of color you want. Remove and drain on paper towels until completely dry.

DECORATED EGGS FOR CHILDREN

styrofoam eggs (optional)
painted or dyed eggs
beads or sequins
glue
felt
scissors
ribbons
basket, to display

If the idea of working with blown eggs sounds too daunting for your children, look for styrofoam eggs in craft shops. These can be painted in just the same way, then decorated when dry.

Alternatively, you could use your already dyed eggs. They will still have two holes at the top and bottom which will need covering up. Choose some attractive beads that are slightly larger than the holes and spread glue round the edge of the underside. Position them carefully over the holes so that no gap is left showing and gently press down.

Try gluing on beads and cut felt shapes in contrasting colors. Felt can also be bought with an adhesive backing, making the project even easy for young children.

Rather than using felt, you could glue thin strips of ribbon or rickrack trimming round your eggs, and you could use sequins rather than beads.

Arrange the decorated eggs in a pretty basket for all to see.

EASTER BASKET

wicker basket

small vase with a selection
   of spring flowers, or a
   potted plant with lots of
   flower heads

tissue paper

moss

decorated blown eggs

For a traditional rustic look, choose a wicker basket large enough to hold either a small vase of cut flowers or a potted plant without the container showing over the rim of the basket. Choose a selection of spring flowers, their stems cut short, or a plant with lots of flower heads.

Use tissue paper round the vase or plant pot to provide packing and keep it stable, then top with moss. Arrange your decorated blown eggs so they nestle in the moss around the flowers and you will now have a beautiful centerpiece for your Easter table.

KIDS' EASTER BASKETS

one 11 x 16½ in. piece of
   light lilac card
one 11 x 16½ in. piece of
   dark lilac card
20 inches lilac gingham
   ribbon
glue
transparent sticky tape
hole punch
1 pack of pink shredded
   tissue paper
mixed candy

Children will love these colorful baskets filled with all their favorite candy.

Begin by cutting 2 circles of light lilac card with a radius of 2½ inches. Then cut 15 vertical strips from the light lilac card 1 x 8 inches. Fold each one in half lengthways and then fold up by ½ inch in the same direction at each end. Attach the folded strip to one of the cut circles with glue by over-lapping the ½ inch fold on the top and bottom of the circle, so that it is sandwiched in between. Repeat this for each strip around the circle to form a flower shape. Then, fold up all of the strips so that they are standing vertically—the circle will now act as the base of the basket.

Cut 3 horizontal strips of dark lilac card measuring 1 x 18 inches. Thread these through the vertical strips one at a time to form the weave of the basket.

Glue the second circle of light lilac card to the base of the basket to tidy up and secure the insides of the basket with transparent sticky tape if necessary.

Punch 2 holes on either side of the basket. Cut the ribbon to a length of your choice and thread through the holes to make a handle. Tie in a loose knot or bow at either side.

Fill the basket with shredded tissue paper and mixed candy of your choice. You could also attach a name tag to the handle and use these baskets as individual place settings for a children's party.

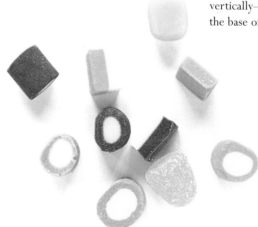

FLORAL CENTERPIECE

chunky square or rectangular
  vase
double-sided sticky tape
fresh or dry moss
raffia
spring flowers, to fill vase

If you are planning a get-together for family and friends over the Easter holiday, the chances are you will be sitting down to a big meal at some point. With florists' shops full of beautifully colored and perfumed spring flowers, now is the time to create an attractive floral centerpiece for your table.

For the most dramatic effect, choose a chunky square or rectangular glass vase so you can see as much of the flowers as possible. Fix some double-sided tape in a strip around the outside of the vase. Buy fresh or dry moss from your florist and fix it to the tape round your vase. Then, tie with raffia to secure in place.

Now simply fill the vase with a selection of your favorite spring flowers, such as tulips, daffodils or crocuses.

EGG TREE

ribbon or cord
needle or fine wire
decorated blown eggs (see
  page 52)
beads, optional
plant foam
galvanized container
pussy willow

This will provide a dramatic room decoration and is also great fun to assemble.

First you will need to thread colored and decorated blown eggs with ribbon or cord. Cut lengths of different colored thin ribbon or decorative cord long enough to go up through the eggs, round the twigs of the egg tree, and down and out through the eggs again. Using a needle or fine wire if you do not have a needle with a large enough eye, take a length of ribbon or cord through each egg. Knot the two tail ends handing below each egg so that the eggs do not fall off. You could also attach wide-eyed beads at the top and bottom of the egg, threading the ribbon or cord through them before hanging and knotting.

Place plant foam at the bottom of a galvanized container and arrange pussy willow or other twigs in it to make an interesting display. The foam will keep them stable when the colored eggs are attached. Interestingly, a shiny new galvanized container will acquire an attractive matte surface if it is left outside for a few weeks prior to use.

INDEX

Photographer: Stephen Conroy
Juliet Piddington endpapers, 6, 8, 15, 32, 51, 58
Food Stylist: David Morgan